Senior Citizens Abuse in India

And What to do About it

Siva Prasad Bose

pencil

ISBN 978-93-5610-223-1

Published in India 2022 by Pencil

Contributors:
Co-Author: Joy Bose

A brand of
One Point Six Technologies Pvt. Ltd.
123, Building J2, Shram Seva Premises,
Wadala Truck Terminal, Wadala (E)
Mumbai 400037, Maharashtra, INDIA
E connect@thepencilapp.com
W www.thepencilapp.com

Author biography

Siva Prasad Bose is an electrical engineer by profession. He is currently retired after many years of service in Uttar Pradesh Power Corporation Limited. He received his engineering degree from Jadavpur University, Kolkata and has a law degree from Meerut University, Meerut. His interests lie in the fields of family law, civil law, law of contracts, and any areas of law related to power electricity related issues.

Joy Bose is a software engineer and a data scientist by profession.

CONTENTS

Preface

Abuse of senior citizens is often an unspoken issue in India. Compared to other kinds of abuse, senior citizen abuse is unique in the fact that it often happens within the same household in which the senior citizens are staying, the abusers are family members on whom the person is dependent and most often the abuses go unreported.

Even though traditionally Indian culture promotes respect for senior citizens, with the changing lifestyles and moving away from joint families and even nuclear families, abuse has become a big issue. Some people may treat their senior citizen parents or family members as a burden and not look after them well, others may be more interested in their property to which they may hold the title, and ill treat them in order to get rights to the property. This problem may be becoming worse because of the Covid pandemic, since senior citizens may be less mobile, less familiar with apps and services and also scared to move out for fear of catching the disease.

Moreover, senior citizens are often scared psychologically of courts and police and may be unfamiliar with laws protecting them, in case of abuses. Lack of familiarity with technology is another big problem, since many of the protections depend on access to the internet and filing online complaints at various web portals and senior citizen helplines. Because of all this, senior citizens even if they face abuse are reluctant or not able to report it.

Although laws and institutions do exist in India to prevent abuse and provide relief to senior citizens, in practice there may be lack of awareness of such laws, also it may be difficult for senior citizens to access these protections due to reasons mentioned. Hence, in this book we focus on the practical steps that a senior citizen or their well-wishers need to take to obtain support and protection.

Important Law Books/ References Consulted

• Maintenance and Welfare of Parents and Senior Citizens Act, 2007 (Bare Act) – 2020 by LexisNexis

• Maintenance & Welfare of Parents & Senior Citizens Act, 2007 – 1 January 2015 by Professional Book Publishers

• The Maintenance and Welfare of Parents and Senior Citizens Act, 2007 – 1 January 2019 by Sathpal Puliani (Author, Editor)

• Elder Abuse and Legal Protection by Dr. Harpreet Kaur. Central Law Publications

• Criminal Procedure Code 1973 Volume 1 and 2 by Durga Das Basu. LexisNexis

• Reports by HelpAge India and AgeWell Foundation

Acknowledgements

Important Law Books/ References Consulted

• Maintenance and Welfare of Parents and Senior Citizens Act, 2007 (Bare Act) – 2020 by LexisNexis

• Maintenance & Welfare of Parents & Senior Citizens Act, 2007 – 1 January 2015 by Professional Book Publishers

• The Maintenance and Welfare of Parents and Senior Citizens Act, 2007 – 1 January 2019 by Sathpal Puliani (Author, Editor)

• Elder Abuse and Legal Protection by Dr. Harpreet Kaur. Central Law Publications

• Criminal Procedure Code 1973 Volume 1 and 2 by Durga Das Basu. LexisNexis

• Reports by HelpAge India and AgeWell Foundation

What is senior citizens abuse

Abuse can be defined as cruel or violent treatment of any person that is intended to harm that person, especially when coming from a person who is trusted. When the person being abused by someone (the abuser) is a senior citizen, it can be termed as elderly abuse or senior citizen abuse. It can be one incident of abuse or multiple repeated incidents. It can also be lack of an action, such as deliberate neglect of the needs of an elderly person. It can take various forms, and effects both male and female senior citizens.

The United Nations and World Health Organizations have highlighted elder abuse, or senior citizens abuse, as a global issue that effects millions of older people around the world. The UN General Assembly passed resolution 66/127, designating June 15 as World Elder Abuse Awareness Day to raise awareness about this problem.

In this chapter, we look at the various types of abuse which senior citizens might face in India.

1.1 Physical abuse

Physical abuse includes physical violence to the body, such as by beating. It can also include other forms of harm such as depriving someone of food or shelter, especially if that person was or is dependent on the abuser. It can take forms such as evicting a senior citizen out of the house where they were residing together with the abuser, neglect by not giving medicines or feeding them bad or stale food or not giving them regular meals altogether.

Senior citizens may be physically weak due to old age and may be helpless to fight back at such abuse, especially from close family members with whom they are living and on whom they are dependent for basic necessities.

1.2 Mental, emotional or psychological abuse

Mental abuse includes various forms of mental or psychological harm to the abused person by the abuser, rather than physical violence. This can take forms such as giving threats, humiliation, insults, verbally abusing the senior citizen, deliberately not listening to their concerns, deliberately doing actions to make their daily life difficult in various cruel ways such as depriving them of basics like water or electricity and so on. It can also take forms like forced confinement or isolation. Emotional abuse can also take the form of emotional blackmail.

The long-term effect of such abuse is to deprive the abused person of their self-esteem and well-being. It can lead to effects such as depression and other mental health issues in the senior citizens subjected to such abuse.

1.3 Neglect and dependency related abuse

Many senior citizens are dependent on their grown children, particularly on their sons and daughters, including daughters in law who are living with them. They may not have fixed incomes since they are no longer able to work as in their youth, even though the property may be in their name. So they may be dependent on others for basics such as food, water, clothing, housing etc. In some cases, the senior citizens might have some income from their pension but still might be dependent for other necessities such as food and medical care.

This kind of dependency situation can be used to abuse the senior citizen by depriving them of the things they are dependent on. This can take the form of neglect. Neglect of senior citizens can take different forms, such as not caring for them properly, not providing them proper food and medicines in a timely fashion, not ensuring proper medical treatment as per their needs, not providing proper emotional care or respect, and so on.

1.4 Financial and property related abuse

Financial abuse can take forms such as not supporting the senior citizen financially with respect to their basic needs, stealing the financial or other property of the senior citizens, or forcing them to turn over their property or financial assets to the abuser. This kind of abuse is more common when the perpetrator is a family member or close relative, even the son or daughter, of the persons being abused.

The abusers may feel that the senior citizens are too weak or vulnerable to fight back, so it is a good time to snatch or steal their property by hook or by crook. Or they may confine the senior citizen persons, in whose name the property belongs, to a small room in an isolated section of the property, neglect them, and themselves with their family occupy most of the rooms.

In India, abuse related to property is a common source of abuse for senior citizens, as per multiple surveys by HelpAge India.

Many senior citizens in India are even destitute or homeless, and are in the streets or slums. They also face abuse from various sections of society because of their destitution.

1.5 Abuse in old age homes

There are many senior citizens in India who are staying in old age homes. They might have reached there because of a variety of reasons including by their own choice, put there by their children who might be unwilling or have no time to take care of them, or because they have been destitute and picked up by some charity organizations or NGOs and put into the old age homes.

Even inside the old age homes, especially in underfunded ones, senior citizens might be subjected to abuse by cruel or unqualified nurses and caregivers. This might even include sexual abuse.

Problems faced by senior citizens

In this chapter we study some data related to abuse of senior citizens, to throw some light on the extent of the problem.

India has a huge population of senior citizens, with them making up about 8% of the Indian population of more than a billion. Out of this, more than 135 million people are elderly senior citizens above 80 years of age.

There have been a few studies and surveys on the problems of senior citizens in India related to abuse. They are listed in the following subsections.

2.1 Senior citizens abuse within the family

In an article in PTI, based on a study by AgeWell Foundation, it was reported that about 71% of the senior citizens have been harassed or humiliated by their own family members and relatives. However, they rarely report the abuse, mostly out of ignorance of the process or law, along with fear of reprisals. Also, since they may be living with and dependent on the abusers, there is a possibility of the abuse becoming worse if they complain about it to others.

Sources:

• Annual report 2017-18, AgeWell Foundation, http://www.agewellfoundation.org/wp-content/uploads/2018/07/Annual_Report-2017-18.pdf

• Agewell Foundation, 2014, Human Rights of Older People in India: A reality check. https://social.un.org/ageing-working-group/documents/fifth/AgewellFoundationHumanRightsofOlderPeopleinIndia.pdf

• Press Trust of India, June 2019. Over 71 pc senior citizens in India victims of abuse by family members: Survey. https://economictimes.indiatimes.com/news/politics-and-nation/over-71-pc-senior-citizens-in-india-victims-of-abuse-by-family-members-survey/articleshow/69777963.cms?from=mdr

• World Health Organization, Elder Abuse in India, country Report. https://www.who.int/ageing/projects/elder_abuse/alc_ea_ind.pdf?ua=1

Another study by Helpage India, highlighted in an article in the Hindu newspaper, found that daughters in law abuse the elderly most (44%), followed by their own daughters (32%) and then their sons (24%). The same study also found that only 24% of the abused senior citizens were willing to report the abuse.

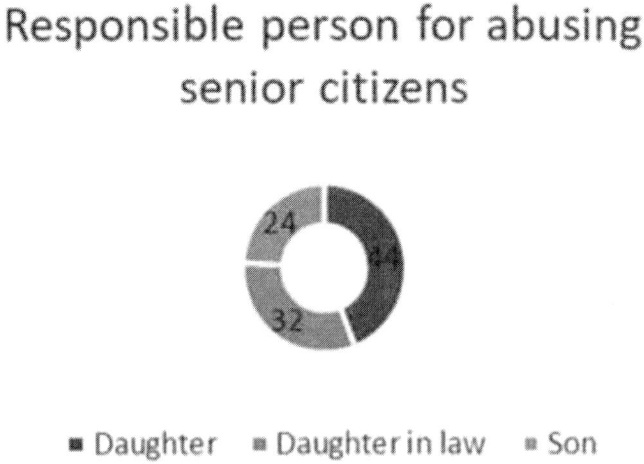

Figure 1: Figure as per the Hindu newspaper article on responsible person for abusing senior citizens, among family members

Source:

- Hindu, June 2013. Daughters-in-law abuse elderly more, says HelpAge India study. https://www.thehindu.com/news/cities/Thiruvananthapuram/daughtersinlaw-abuse-elderly-more-says-helpage-india-study/article4817075.ece

2.2 High cost of medical treatment

Government hospitals in India are often poorly equipped, so many senior citizens prefer to go to private hospitals. However, the cost of treatment in such private hospitals is very expensive. For example, there were reports of ICU beds of Covid patients in 2020 being charged at Rupees 80000 per day, 9 lakhs for ICU with ventilator treatment for 10 days in some private hospitals in the big cities. Therefore, one must go for health insurance to help pay the cost of such treatment.

Most private health insurance in India is aimed at younger people. Private health insurance for senior citizens above 65 is often unaffordable, with premiums running into Rs 20000 per year or more. This results in many senior citizens not having adequate health cover. Even for those senior citizens whose children are working in the corporate sector, many private companies do not cover the medical insurance for parents. Also, if one leaves the company or is fired, the medical insurance coverage from the employer may be cut off suddenly. Another problem is insurance providers suddenly hiking the insurance premiums after a few years.

Government health insurance schemes such as Ayushman Bharat often leave out most middle-class people including senior citizens.

Source:

- Economic Times, Nov 2019. Are independent health insurance covers for seniors unaffordable? Here's what experts say. https://economictimes.indiatimes.com/wealth/insure/health-insurance/are-independent-health-insurance-covers-for-seniors-unaffordable-heres-what-experts-say/articleshow/71982283.cms?from=mdr

2.3 Poverty and homelessness in senior citizens

Millions of elderly people in India are living below the poverty line and have no income security, found a report.

Similarly, many of the senior citizens in India are homeless, since they are abandoned by their children. A few lucky ones, with enough money to pay for it, languish in old age homes.

Source:

- IANS and Financial Express, June 2017. As India ages, over 61% of elderly will have no income security by 2050 https://www.financialexpress.com/economy/as-india-ages-over-61-of-elderly-will-have-no-income-security-by-2050/717511/

2.4 Problems related to property disputes

Many senior citizens might have property in their name, bought during their working life. However, they may have grown up children who are living with them and taking care of the property, and who are desirous of getting hold of the property from their parents as soon as possible. The same holds for other relatives in the extended family, who may perceive the senior citizens as weak and as soft targets, from whom it would be relatively easy to snatch the property.

In a survey, it was reported that about 48% of senior citizens in India were trapped in one or more property related disputes, including revoking of their will. The same survey showed that 58 per cent petitioners faced physical abuse (beating and hitting), 28 per cent suffered mental torture.

In another survey reported in the Hindu newspaper, it was reported that 57% of calls to the elders helpline number in Bangalore were related to intra familial issues including property disputes.

Sources:

• PTI, Jan 2018. 48 per cent senior citizens involved in property-related disputes: Survey. https://housing.com/news/48-per-cent-senior-citizens-involved-property-related-disputes-survey/

• Hindustan Times, Jul 2018. Abuse of elderly for property: A house divided by greed. https://www.hindustantimes.com/punjab/abuse-of-elderly-for-property-a-house-divided-by-greed/story-vwLYHVC6bZqNYjWrsdNBFI.html

• The Hindu, June 2014. Intra-familial elder abuse attributed to property disputes. https://www.thehindu.com/news/cities/bangalore/intrafamilial-elder-abuse-attributed-to-property-disputes/article6115215.ece

2.5 Isolation due to Covid lockdown

In another survey published in TOI, 71% of senior citizens said their abuse has increased due to the Covid pandemic and its subsequent lockdown. During the pandemic, many senior citizens would be more reluctant to get out of the house for fear of catching Covid and being a more vulnerable group. This would lead to lack of physical activity, increased isolation, bringing with it an increased amount of domestic abuse and all kinds of mental health related problems.

Source:

- Times of India, June 2020. Abuse has increased during lockdown, say 71 percent of elderly. https://timesofindia.indiatimes.com/india/abuse-has-increased-during-lockdown-say-71-of-elderly/articleshow/76377324.cms

2.6 Lack of access to technology

Many senior citizens, especially from the middle class or lower middle class and those who are in small cities, might be unfamiliar with technology including digital payments. Similarly, some senior citizens might be old fashioned and prefer small and personal kinara stores as opposed to the modern malls.

For such people, increased modernization and digitalization might cause more problems and inconvenience. They might be unable to use digital services like Uber and digital money transfers like Paytm. They may not even know how to use ATMs and credit cards.

All these problems may be even worse in case of female senior citizens especially those who are housewives, as their interaction with wider society is further limited.

2.7 Lack of empathy from various service providers

Lack of empathy, understanding and patience from various service providers in India can also be a contributing factor to increasing the problems of senior citizens. In places like supermarkets, ticket booking offices, banks or government offices, the employees may not have been provided training specifically to be senior citizen friendly. This can lead to lack of understanding from such employees who are already stressed and pressed for time, leading to difficulties when senior citizens try to access their services.

The same holds for institutions meant for their protection, such as police and judiciary in some cases. Senior citizens may find it difficult to raise their complaints against abuse or to seek relief, given the slow moving, bureaucratized and sometimes corrupt judiciary, police and other institutions. In some cases, they may not know of fast changing latest procedures and hence might be ignored or ill-treated by the service providers. The problem can be even worse if their abusers turn out to have political or other connections.

2.8 Crimes report by National Crimes Records Bureau (NCRB)

National Crimes Records Bureau or NCRB is the Indian government agency responsible for collecting and compiling statistics on all kinds of crimes reported to the police. They file annual reports containing breakdown of crimes under different categories. Since senior citizens are usually reluctant to approach the police, the crime statistics against senior citizens suffers from underreporting. The statistics mostly include financial and other crimes by strangers such as dacoity, robbery and murder, and ignore the crimes committed by persons within the same household, which are the most common form of senior citizens abuse but are very difficult to report.

Sources:

- NCRB, Crime in India 2019 report. Website: https://ncrb.gov.in/en/crime-india-2019-0

- Volume 2 of the 2019 NCRB report contains a breakdown of crimes against senior citizens: https://ncrb.gov.in/sites/default/files/CII%202019%20Volume%202.pdf

- NCRB, Crimes against senior citizens, 2015 report https://ncrb.gov.in/sites/default/files/crime_in_india_table_additional_table_chapter_reports/Chapter%2020-15.11.16_2015.pdf

Real life examples of senior citizen abuse

In this chapter we go through a few real-life examples to give an idea of how senior citizen abuse is prevalent in our society.

3.1 Newspaper clippings

Below are some extracts from recent newspaper clippings:

3.1.1 Example where video is shared of a senior citizen being severely abused by her own son

The New Indian Express, 30 December 2020: Man arrested after video of him brutally torturing mother goes viral

THIRUVANANTHAPURAM: After the back-to-back videos from Neyyattinkara where a couple had accidentally set themselves ablaze over a land dispute, a new video has emerged from Kerala that's shocked the conscience of the public. Sitting on the floor and leaning against the wall, Shahida, a woman in her late fifties, is taking blows on her face. Her shrieks and loud prayers notwithstanding, the attacker keeps on slapping her and throwing kicks on her face and ribs. A feeble female voice can be heard uttering something which suggests "I am not going to interfere." Apparently, it's this woman, who is shooting the video. As the video went viral, Ayiroor police registered a suo motu case and arrested Razaq. The police said the incident happened a month back and the victim had then refused to lodge a complaint. Razaq was working as a private bus cleaner and is said to be a drug addict.

3.1.2 Example where a senior citizen was evicted out of her house by her sons over property

Mirror Now Digital. Dec 6 2020. Humanity evicted: 99-year-old mother thrown out of house after being physically, mentally tortured by 4 sons

Bhopal: A 99-year-old mother was allegedly forced to spend two days on the road two months ago after her four sons threw out of the house in Madhya Pradesh. The incident came to fore after the elderly woman, an Ashok Nagar city resident, moved the Bhopal district court last week, seeking Rs 10,000 as monthly maintenance allowance from her sons and a right to live respectfully until death.

Elderly woman alleges torture by sons: The nonagenarian stated that she had six sons of whom the eldest died, while the youngest is differently-abled. She had been staying with the other four sons – two are government servants and two make a living from farming – since her husband's death in 2001. "After the death of my husband in 2001, my four sons encroached upon the whole property, including an 8-acre agricultural land and a house in Ashok Nagar. They cursed and harassed me. They starved me. I have been tortured physically and mentally for the past few years," a report by Hindustan Times quoted the elderly mother as saying.

3.1.3 Example where a senior citizen couple were beaten up by neighbors over a property dispute

Mumbai Mirror, Sep 19, 2016. Wadala elderly couple beaten up by neighbor

Refusal to sell their flat prompted assault, alleges couple; accused counters with assault complaint of his own

Mumbai: A fight between two neighbors in Wadala took an ugly turn when two senior citizens were beaten up with hockey sticks at their residence in Kidwai Colony and ended up with fractures and stitches. Haroon Siddiqui, 75, and Zarina Siddiqui, 68, were rushed to KEM Hospital where Haroon received five stitches and is being treated for four fractures while Zarina received 15 stitches. Police sources said that the two families have been locked in a dispute over the Siddiqui's ground-floor apartment for more than two years now as the Khan family – accused by the Siddiquis of attacking them – has been wanting to purchase it despite Zarina and Haroon's refusal.

3.1.4 Example where a senior citizen was beaten up by son and daughter in law for demanding maintenance amount

Sambad. Oct 14, 2019: Beaten Up By Son, Daughter-In-Law, Elderly Woman Seeks Police Help

Phulbani: The value of maternal love seems to have declined with domination of money for which old age appears to be a curse for many in modern society. Here's a heart-rending incident reported from Phulbani town of Kandhamal district where a 70-year-old woman was beaten up by her son and daughter-in-law over a sum of money. Being tortured and humiliated by children, the victim approached police seeking justice at old age. According to reports, the elderly couple Utsab Nayak and Kuntala Nayak of Amalapada area has three sons and one daughter. However, they are staying with daughter as their sons expressed disinterest to keep parents with them. As part of their responsibility towards parents, the sons were paying some money to them every month.

Sources said that the second son Ramesh Nayak of the couple had not paid his part of money in past two months for which Kuntala had visited his home to know the reason. When she asked his son for money, the latter along with his wife started assaulting her physically in front of home. Later, the duo dragged the old woman into the house and beat her up without mercy for demanding money.

3.2 Examples from reports

Below are some extracts from reports by Agewell and HelpAge India.

3.2.1 Extracts from a report on Elder Abuse by HelpAge India

HelpAge India. Elder Abuse in India 2014 Chapter 4, Personal Experience of Abuse:

Across the cities, 50% of the elders admitted to having personally experienced abuse, though 83% of all elders surveyed, are of the view that it is prevalent in society. Across the cities, Verbal Abuse (41 %), Disrespect (33%) and Neglect (29%) were the major types of abuse faced by the elderly. Elders across cities were asked about the abusers within their family. The Daughter-in-law (61%) and Son

(59%) emerged as the topmost perpetrators. This is a trend that is continuing from the previous years. Not surprisingly, 77% of those surveyed, live with their families. Across the cities, 'Emotional dependence on the abuser' (46%) and 'Economic dependence on the abuser' (45%) are the major reasons for them being abused. Among those who experienced abuse, 41% did not report the abuse to anyone. The elderly who were abused, but, did not report were asked about the reasons for the same. The majority stated that they wanted "To maintain confidentiality of family matter" (59%). 17 %"Did not know how to deal with the problem." The highest awareness of a Redressal Mechanism is the Police Helplines at 64%, 14% are aware of the Maintenance Act and 9% are even aware of the HelpAge India Elder Helplines. However, 18% are not aware of any mechanism.

HelpAge India. Elder Abuse in India 2014 Chapter 5. Beaten in body, mind and spirit. The dark stories of Elder Abuse in India

From Bengaluru: economic exploitation by Abuser "They want my money and so they abuse me"

Ramaiah (name changed), is a 67 year old from ITI Colony in Bengaluru. He has a rental income which is good enough to take care of his and his wife's needs. However, his son and daughter in law want this money for themselves and constantly abuse the couple over it. Ramiah's deteriorating health and the resultant medical expenses force him to keep the money to meet this need. This caused many a friction between him and his son and daughter in law so much so that the he and wife chose to live separately and face life by themselves. His relatives were no help in resolving the issue as they merely laughed at

Ramaiah's family problems. Today, he finds solace in the fact that his wife is by his side.

- Source: https://www.helpageindia.org/wp-content/themes/helpageindia/pdf/elderabuseindia14.pdf

3.2.2 Extracts from a report on Human Rights of Elderly in India by AgeWell Foundation

Agewell Foundation. Human Rights of the Elderly in India: a Critical Reflection on Social Development. July 2015

In all, 2/3rd respondents i.e. 65.2% elderly respondents claimed that older persons face neglect in old age. More than half (54.1%) respondents said that older persons suffer elder abuse in their families/society. Every third elderly claimed that elderly face domestic violence (physical/verbal) in old age. Every fourth elderly, i.e. 25.3% elderly admit that older persons are being exploited by their family members. In all, 89.7% respondents out of 2705 respondents facing elder abuse reportedly said that elderly face mistreatment in old age mostly due to financial reasons. In all, 96.4% of elderly abused respondents claimed that they face mistreatment due to emotional factors. In all, 67.5% of elderly abused respondents said that they face physical elder abuse in general. According to 25% elderly respondents younger generations consider elderly family members as burden on their family. Equal number of elderly (25%) said that generation gap is the main reason behind violation of human rights of older persons In all, 20% elderly respondents admit that their younger family members are unable to take care of their elderly family members.

- Source: https://www.agewellfoundation.org/pdf/reports/Human%20Rights%20of%20Elderly%20in%20India%20-%20A%20Critical%20Reflection%20on%20Social%20Development%20-%20July%202015.pdf

Reasons for senior citizen abuse

Having seen the statistics related to the problem of senior citizen abuse, in this chapter we go through some of the possible reasons behind this abuse, and why senior citizens specifically are more vulnerable.

4.1 Economic reasons

With the changing society and rising unemployment especially during the pandemic, coupled with rising inflation, many young people may not have the means to take care of senior citizens in India. The high costs of medical insurance and treatment further add to the problem of making senior citizens feel like a burden to young people.

4.2 Lack of a comprehensive social welfare system

Unlike developed countries such as European countries, India has a very small or non-existent welfare system for senior citizens. Therefore, government help is very less and difficult to find, especially for middle class senior citizen people who might be earning a little more than the threshold for getting access to economically weak schemes of the government.

4.3 Reasons with married children

Married people may feel that they have their own family to support, so why bother with their old parents. Sometimes they face pressure from the wider society and wives to dedicate their salary and resources to their own family and not to their parents, and also to live separately from their parents.

4.4 Changing lifestyles in cities

In the west, it is typical for young people to leave their parents' homes at 16 and move out, there is also no tradition of taking care of parents in their old age. Indians sometimes tend to ape the west and Western society, disregarding our traditional respect for old people. So this is becoming a common trend in India too, especially with modernization.

4.5 Children who are working migrants

With the advent of modern lifestyles, the joint families of old (which used to act like welfare systems for elders in the joint family) have all but disappeared. Many times, the husband and wife with their kids have to move to a different city to work, which is far away from the native place where the senior citizen parents live.

Such problems of senior citizen mistreatment and abuse are common with all levels of Indian society: with the middle-class white-collar IT workers who are working in IT firms in IT hub cities like Bangalore or Gurgaon as well as migrant laborers.

4.6 Lack of awareness in society and media

Mass media such as TV and newspapers rarely focus on the problems of senior citizens. They may even show them in a negative light, such as in soap operas and films.

Therefore, given this kind of problems, the problem of senior citizen abuse becomes widespread and also gets very little attention from the wider society. Hence, it becomes more important to raise awareness of such kinds of problems and the available remedies.

4.7 Domestic Disputes

Sometimes domestic disputes, such as between the daughters in law and senior citizen parents, can also become a cause of abuse. Sometimes, the husband and wife cannot get along, or else the mother-in-law and daughter-in-law cannot get along. Often in such cases, the men start living separately or else there is neglect and abuse of the old parents in law. The HelpAge study in the Hindu article mentioned in the previous chapter found that daughters in law abused the elderly in 44% of the cases. The root causes of this could be changing cultures, inter generation gap, and other social issues in India.

Where to go for help

In this chapter, we go through some of the avenues and organizations where senior citizens, or those concerned for their welfare, can go for help and protection in case of abuse.

5.1 Local police station

The most natural place for senior citizens to go to in case of abuse is their local police station. It is the duty of the police to help vulnerable people in society such as senior citizens. The police can be reached wither by calling the special emergency telephone number 100 or by visiting the police station to register a police complaint, after which they may file an FIR.

However, this is the very place many senior citizens may be most reluctant to go to, either for fear of the police, fear of the process of reporting abuse or fear of repercussions from the abusers who may be their own family members on whom they are dependent. Sometimes in India, especially in smaller cities, the police may be corrupt or ask for bribes, or be reluctant to lodge an FIR to avoid extra work for themselves. Also, some senior citizens might equate going to the police with bringing shame on their family and so would be extra reluctant to report the abuse. Others might feel that their family members might be jailed by the police if they report the abuse incident, even though in practice this is very unlikely to happen, and so do not report the abuse incidents.

5.2 Senior citizen cells and helplines

In some big cities, there may exist some special helplines to report incidents of abuse. Sometimes, the local police themselves may set up such helplines. Senior citizens can call these helpline numbers in case of abuse, and they connect to a specialized police cell. All such helpline calls are usually logged, so chances of getting justice using these helplines is better. However, such senior citizen cells and helplines are not available in all cities, only in the big metro cities. The phone number 1090 is applicable for most senior citizen helplines, so it is worth trying this number.

Example Senior Citizen helpline numbers are as follows:

- 1091/1291 of Delhi Police Senior Citizen Helpline
- 1090 Elders helpline of Bangalore police.

5.3 Senior citizens tribunals

The Senior citizen tribunal is constituted for appeals related to Senior Citizens Act 2007. Such tribunals are available in many big cities in India and are usually under the district magistrate (DM) or the additional district magistrate (ADM). The senior citizen should approach the DMs or ADMs with a written complaint, in order to get the relief.

The Senior Citizens Protection Act, also called the Maintenance and Welfare of Parents and Senior Citizens Act, 2007, can be invoked by senior citizens to ask the courts or police for maintenance from their children and legal heirs in case they are destitute or homeless, or face threats to their life and well-being. However, the process of seeking redressal under this act can sometimes be complicated, the senior citizens might have to approach the courts for the purpose, which can be daunting.

Some links to senior citizen tribunals are as follows:

- Delhi Senior Citizens Tribunal: https://socialwelfare.delhigovt.nic.in/content/district-maintenance-tribunal-officers

- Bangalore Senior Citizens Tribunal: https://www.kaanoon.com/127612/details-of-senior-citizen-s-tribunal-in-bangalore

5.4 National Human Rights Commission (NHRC)

In cases where some government servant, such as police or others, are involved in the abuse, senior citizens file an online complaint at the National Human Rights Commission or NHRC, either online or in person, by visiting their office or by writing a letter and sending by registered post. There are also similar state human rights commissions in different stats of India.

However, the NHRC platform is mostly based online, so it might be difficult for senior citizens to use it if they are not adequately familiar with technology.

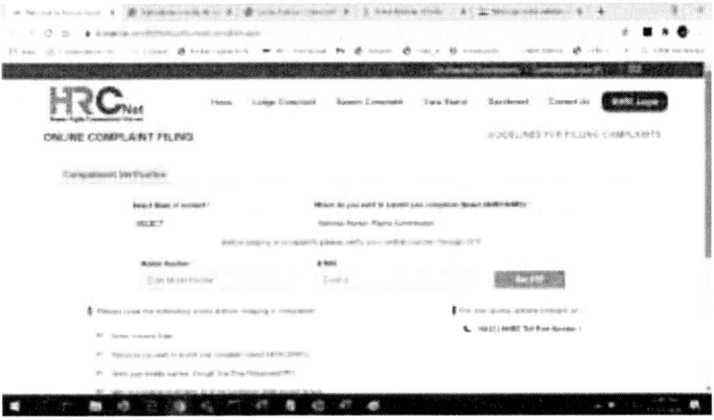

Figure 2: Interface for filing online complaints at the NHRC website

The NHRC website for how to file an online complaint and the complaints portal is as follows: https://nhrc.nic.in/complaints/complaints/how-to-file-a-complaints and https://www.hrcnet.nic.in/HRCNet/public/webcomplaint.aspx

5.5 National Commission for Women

NCW or National Commission for Women Cell is primarily meant for protecting women facing domestic violence and other kinds of abuse. It can, therefore, also help senior citizen women. The NCW website has a space for logging online complaints of abuse by women. The complaints first go through a verification process before they are accepted and given a registration number.

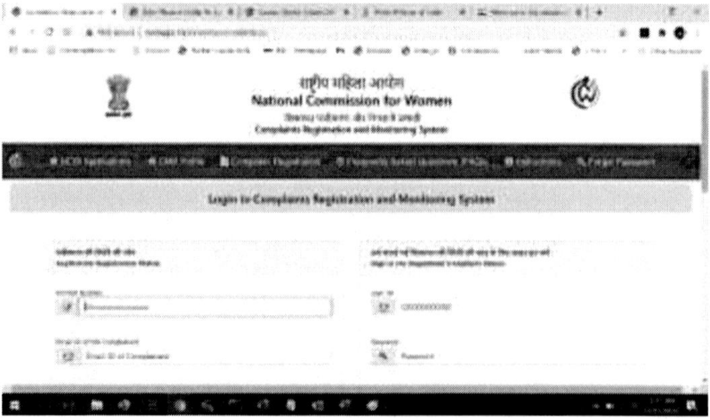

Figure 3: Interface for filing online complaints at the NCW website

The NCW website for logging online complaints is at the following link: http://ncwapps.nic.in/onlinecomplaintsv2/

5.6 Senior citizen NGOs

Senior Citizen NGOs: There are a few NGOs focused on helping senior citizens, both nationally and in different cities, such as HelpAge India, Dignity Foundation, Agewell Foundation, Harmony. We will study them in detail in a coming chapter. Such NGOs can be a useful support group for senior citizens, as they might give a sympathetic hearing to them and also connect them with the local police, old age homes and other services.

The websites of some of these NGOs are as follows:

• Helpage India: https://www.helpageindia.org/

• Dignity Foundation. https://dignityfoundation.com/

• Agewell Foundation https://www.agewellfoundation.org/

• Harmony https://www.harmonyindia.org/

5.7 Local MPs, MLAs and other politicians

In some cases, though not all cases, the local politicians might be able to help in case of abuse. The senior citizens or their well-wishers should find out the contacts or offices of the local politicians and visit them or write letters to highlight their situation and asking for help or protection.

• The website https://www.contactminister.com/ has the contact details of various members of parliament in India

- The website https://www.india.gov.in/my-government/whos-who/mlasmlcs gives a list of all the MLAs in different states of India.

5.8 Local or national newspapers

Another possible avenue for senior citizens to highlight their issues is the print and digital media, such as local newspapers in English, Hindi or regional languages. Many of these newspapers have a space for readers to send letters to the editor, either physical letters or by email. Generally, the email addresses for writing to the editor are mentioned in the newspapers in the same place where the letters are published. The writer should mention his or her full name, mailing address and subject of the letter.

For some example newspapers, the contacts are as follows:

- The Hindu newspaper, the email address for letters to the editor is letters@thehindu.co.in

- The email for Hindustan Times is letters@hindustantimes.com and Hindustan (Hindi newspaper) is mailbox@livehindustan.com

However, this avenue of writing to Indian newspapers is more likely to succeed if the letters highlight the social problem of senior citizens abuse in more general terms, along with what can be done as a society to stop such incidents.

5.9 Old age homes

In case of severe issues such as homelessness due to being abandoned by their children, senior citizens may try to contact old age homes.

Source:

• Rhythm Sachdeva, Give India, October 2019. 10 old age homes in India for abandoned senior citizens https://blog.giveindia.org/elderly/10-old-age-homes-in-india-for-abandoned-senior-citizens/

• Senior Indian. List of old age homes in India (State wise). https://www.seniorindian.com/old_age_homes_list.htm

• Dada Dadi Organization. Directory of old age homes in India. http://dadadadi.org/old-age-homes-in-India.html

5.10 Free or Low cost legal advice websites

There are a number of websites available for getting free or low cost legal advice from lawyers in India. These can be used by senior citizens in case of need. However, they do require familiarity with technology to log their question online.

The procedure to log a legal query is as follows: one has to visit the website, create a free account by filling some basic details. After that, one can log one's query, which will be answered by the lawyers within a few hours. Some of the advocates may send private messages or directly call the person logging the complaint, rather than replying on the public forum. Also, they may ask for a fee for their advice.

Examples include the following:

• Lawrato: https://lawrato.com/free-legal-advice

• Indian Kanoon https://www.kaanoon.com/

• Vkeel https://www.vkeel.com/

• Vidhikarya https://www.vidhikarya.com/

Figure 4: Screenshot for a complaint related to senior citizen abuse logged on the lawrato website

Of these, Lawrato seems to have many lawyers relying to each query promptly and in the public. Indian Kanoon is a very good resource for accessing past court judgements on various topics.

5.11 Prime Minister's Office and President's Secretariat

The senior citizens can also directly approach the prime minister's office with their complaints and grievances.

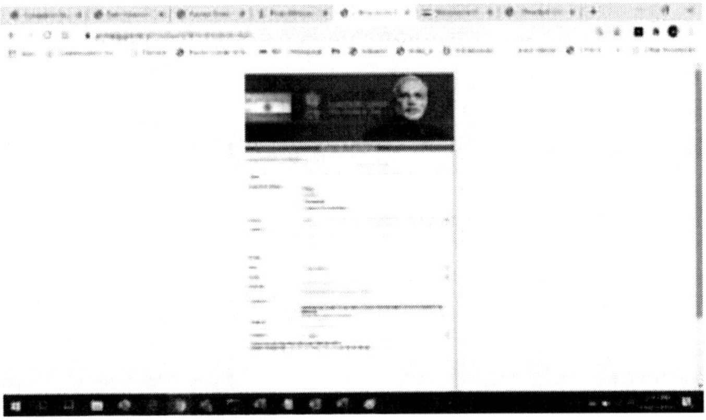

Figure 5: Interface for filing an online grievance at the PMO website

The website to log grievances at the PMO (prime minster office) is as follows: https://pmopg.gov.in/pmocitizen/Grievancepmo.aspx

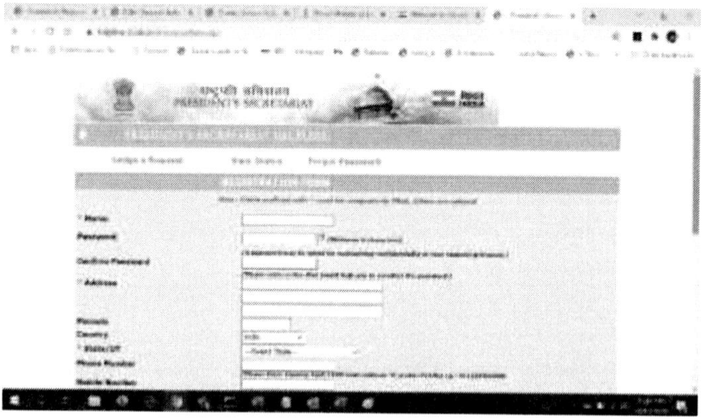

Figure 6: Interface for filing an online request or grievance at the President's secretariat

Similarly, a grievance can be raised with the President's secretariat. The website is as follows: https://helpline.rb.nic.in/GrievanceNew.aspx

5.12 Senior Citizen Associations

Many cities in India have senior citizen associations, where the senior citizens in local communities come together, socialize and discuss their problems. They can be found in both big and small cities. Such organizations can also be a valuable source of support when one is faced with abuse. They often work with NGOs and other organizations to coordinate support to needy senior citizens. It is a good idea for senior citizens to join such organizations.

Some of the associations are as follows:

- All India senior citizens confederation AISCCON: https://www.aisccon.org/

- Senior citizens council of Delhi http://seniorcitizensdelhi.org/

- Senior citizens support forum http://scsforum.org

- Tamil Nadu senior citizens association http://www.tanseca.com/

- Association of senior living India http://www.asli.org.in/

Senior Citizens Protection Act

Senior Citizens Protection Act is also called the Maintenance and Welfare of Parents and Senior Citizens Act, 2007.

In this chapter, we discuss this act and ways to seek redressal by senior citizens who are being abused or neglected by their own children and in a state of poverty. We also discuss some of the state-wise rules for implementation of the act by different states in India.

Maintenance and Welfare of Parents and Senior Citizens Act, 2007

भारत का राजपत्र
The Gazette of India

EXTRAORDINARY

PART II - Section 1

PUBLISHED BY AUTHORITY

MINISTRY OF LAW AND JUSTICE
(Legislative Department)

THE MAINTENANCE AND WELFARE OF PARENTS AND SENIOR CITIZENS ACT, 2007

Figure 7: Cover page of the Senior Citizens Act 2007

6.1 What is covered in the act

The Senior Citizens Protection Act is primarily intended to protect senior citizen parents from abandonment by their family members, and obliges the sons and legal heirs of senior citizens to take care of them by a monthly maintenance allowance. It is enforced by senior citizen tribunals, who can pass maintenance orders.

The act also talks about:

• establishment of old age homes in every district

• provision of medical care by reserving beds for senior citizens in government hospitals

• provisions by respective state governments to be enacted for the protection of life and property of senior citizens.

The first two clauses of the act are as follows:

A senior citizen including parent who is unable to maintain himself from his own earning or property owned by him, shall be entitled to make an application under section 5 in case of –

• parent or grand-parent, against one or more of his children not being a minor

• a childless senior citizen, against such of his relative referred to in clause (g) of section 2

The obligation of the children or relative, as the case may be, to maintain a senior citizen extends to the needs of such citizen so that senior citizen may lead a normal life.

An application for maintenance under section 4, may be made -

• by a senior citizen or a parent, as the case may be; or

• if he is incapable, by any other person or organisation authorised by him; or

• the Tribunal may take cognizance suo motu

6.2 How to approach for help

This act can be invoked by senior citizens by approaching the senior citizen tribunals in their respective state, asking for maintenance from their children or relatives in case of inadequate income to support themselves, loss of residence or other needs.

The maintenance and other protections ordered under this act are to be enforced by senior citizens maintenance tribunals in various cities and in every state, usually under the ADM, SDM or district magistrates.

6.3 Problems with accessing relief under the Senior Citizens act

Even though the senior citizen parents can claim maintenance under the act, the procedure process of seeking redressal under this act can sometimes be time consuming, bureaucratic and expensive. The senior citizens might have to approach the tribunals and sometimes the courts for the purpose of claiming maintenance, which can be daunting. Also, the maintenance amount granted may sometimes be inadequate for supporting the medical and other costs of the senior citizens. Moreover, just granting a certain sum of money and not other kinds of necessary support may not be enough for their needs.

Hence, there is a need to have simpler, inexpensive and speedy provisions to claim maintenance for senior citizen parents.

6.4 Links to more information about the Senior Citizens Protection Act

The following are some links to more information about the act:

- Wikipedia page about the Act https://en.wikipedia.org/wiki/Maintenance_and_Welfare_of_Parents_and_Senior_Citizens_Act,_2007

- Senior Citizens Protection Act soft copy, downloadable as PDF: http://wbja.nic.in/wbja_adm/files/The%20Maintenance%20and%20Welfare%20of%20Parents%20and%20Senior%20Citizens%20Act,%202007.pdf

6.5 Orissa Maintenance of Parents and Senior Citizens Rules, 2009

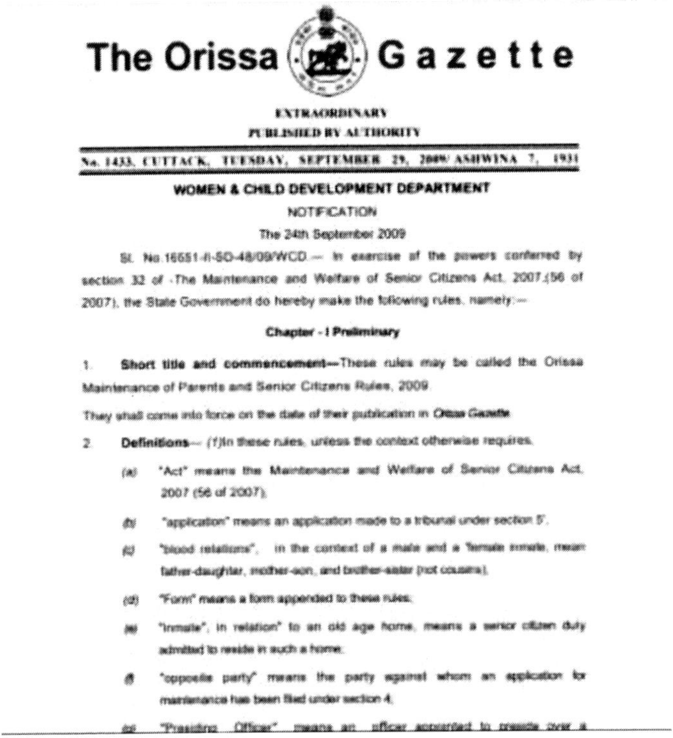

The Orissa Gazette

EXTRAORDINARY
PUBLISHED BY AUTHORITY

No. 1433, CUTTACK, TUESDAY, SEPTEMBER 29, 2009/ ASHWINA 7, 1931

WOMEN & CHILD DEVELOPMENT DEPARTMENT

NOTIFICATION

The 24th September 2009

SL. No.16551-II-SO-48/09/WCD.— In exercise of the powers conferred by section 32 of The Maintenance and Welfare of Senior Citizens Act, 2007 (56 of 2007), the State Government do hereby make the following rules, namely:—

Chapter - I Preliminary

1. **Short title and commencement**—These rules may be called the Orissa Maintenance of Parents and Senior Citizens Rules, 2009.

They shall come into force on the date of their publication in Orissa Gazette.

2. **Definitions**— (1) In these rules, unless the context otherwise requires,

(a) "Act" means the Maintenance and Welfare of Senior Citizens Act, 2007 (56 of 2007);

(b) "application" means an application made to a tribunal under section 5;

(c) "blood relations", in the context of a male and a female inmate, mean father-daughter, mother-son, and brother-sister (not cousins);

(d) "Form" means a form appended to these rules;

(e) "Inmate", in relation to an old age home, means a senior citizen duly admitted to reside in such a home;

(f) "opposite party" means the party against whom an application for maintenance has been filed under section 4;

(g) "Presiding Officer" means an officer appointed to preside over a

Figure 8: Cover page of the Orissa Maintenance of Parents and Senior Citizens Rules 2009

Odisha has a separate set of rules about the procedure for parents to claim maintenance, as per the powers conferred on states in the senior citizens act 2007, which is applicable all over India. These rules are called the Orissa Maintenance of Parents and Senior Citizens Rules, 2009.

- Online version: https://odishapolice.gov.in/sites/default/files/PDF/The

%20Orissa%20Maintenance%20of%20Parents%20%26%20Senior%20Citizens%20Rules%2C2009..pdf

6.6 Karnataka Maintenance of Parents and Senior Citizens Rules, 2009

Karnataka too has specified rules in accordance with the Senior Citizens act 2007. These rules specify the detailed procedures under which to claim maintenance by senior citizen parents and what to do if the respondence do not appear, appeals process, establishment of old age homes and so on.

- The Karnataka rules are available online here: https://www.lawyerservices.in/Karnataka-Maintenance-and-Welfare-of-Parents-and-Senior-Citizens-Rules-2009

6.7 Maharashtra Maintenance of Parents and Senior Citizens Rules, 2010

The Maharashtra state rules are available online here:

- Online version: https://www.latestlaws.com/bare-acts/state-acts-rules/maharashtra-state-laws/maharashtra-maintenance-and-welfare-of-parents-and-senior-citizens-rules-2010/

6.8 Delhi Maintenance and Welfare of Parents and Senior Citizens (Amendment Rules), 2010

- Online version: https://socialwelfare.delhigovt.nic.in/sites/default/files/All-PDF/Rules_0.pdf

6.9 The Assam State Maintenance and Welfare of Parents and Senior Citizens Rules, 2012

- Online version: http://www.bareactslive.com/NER/ner218.htm

6.10 The Andhra Pradesh Maintenance and Welfare of Parents and Senior Citizens Rules, 2011

- Online Version: http://wcdsc.tg.nic.in/documents/maintenance_senior_citizens_act.PDF

6.11 The Kerala Maintenance and Welfare of Parents and Senior Citizens Rules, 2009

- Online version: http://www.bareactslive.com/KER/ker002.htm

Other states also have their own respective versions, although not all may be available online.

Senior citizen helplines

In this chapter, we discuss existing helplines for senior citizens in different cities, set up by the local police or by various charity organizations.

These helplines are ideally supposed to be available 24 hours, but some of them may be operated between 10 am-5 pm or working hours only. A senior citizen who calls these helplines might expect to hear a sympathetic and patient hearing of their problems of abuse, and possible action to help them seek redressal. As such, they are an important means of help for senior citizens who are in urgent trouble or being currently abused by their relatives or neighbors.

7.1 Police helplines against senior citizen abuse

In many but not all cities, 1090 serves as the senior citizen helpline by the police. So even if it is not specifically listed it is worth trying to dial 1090 from any state or city.

- Gujarat Police Help line 1096
- Bengaluru police Senior Citizen Helpline 1090
- Chandigarh Police Senior Citizen Helpline 1090

- Delhi Police Senior Citizen Helpline 1291 and 1091
- Kolkata Police Senior Citizen Helpline 98300 88884
- Mumbai Police Senior Citizen Helpline 1090
- Pune Police Senior Citizen Helpline 1091

These helplines have been a success in providing timely help to senior citizens. In Bangalore, for example, the 1090 helpline run by the city police and Nightingale's Trust gets on average 40 calls daily.

7.2 Delhi police senior citizens cell

Delhi Police has a dedicated senior citizens cell, whom the senior citizens can approach in order to report abuse. This can be used in addition to the helpline number 1291 of the Delhi police.

Senior citizens can directly visit the office and lodge their complaints, or write to them with full details.

The contact details of the delhi police senior citizens cell are as follows:

Delhi Police Senior Citizens Cell

Office : 1st Floor, Police Headquarters,

M.S.O. Building, I.P.Estate, New Delhi.

Website : http://www.delhipolice.nic.in/seniorcitizen/index.html

e-mail : scscphq@bol.net.in

Delhi police also has an app for senior citizens, with an SOS button to contact in case of emergencies. It is meant to help senior citizens who are living alone. They can register their profile on the app or on the Delhi police senior citizen website.

Android store link to the app "Delhi Police Senior Citizen":
https://play.google.com/store/apps/details?id=com.pcsolutions.samparkorsampadan

Figure 9: Screenshots from the Delhi police senior citizens app

7.3 Odisha Police senior citizens security cell

Odisha police has set up senior citizen security cells, along with the 1090 helpline. These cells are set up in all districts of Odisha. Along with other activities, they do verification of domestic servants of senior citizens in the police stations.

The website is https://odishapolice.gov.in/?q=node/6

7.4 List of helplines by Dada Dadi Organization

Dada Dadi organization has a comprehensive list of helplines in various cities, including both the police and voluntary organizations working for senior citizens. Some of these helplines can also provide legal advice when necessary, or put the senior citizen in contact with their lawyer who can help them to file cases in courts.

The link to the helplines is http://dadadadi.org/senior-citizen-helpline.html

The list includes not only the police helplines, but also the ones run by the senior citizen NGOs such as Dignity Foundation, HelpAge India and so on.

Dignity foundation helplines are available in six cities as follows:

- Mumbai Dignity Helpline +91 22 6138 1111

- Chennai Dignity Helpline +91 44 2621 0363

• Kolkata Dignity Helpline +91 92323 82936 / +91 91635 09818

• Bengaluru Dignity Helpline +91 96322 44568 / +91 97405 52261

• Pune Dignity Helpline +91 88304 49043

• Delhi Dignity Helpline +91 84483 17316

The HelpAge India helpline number is 1800-180-1253, which is a toll free number and applicable across India.

Some other helplines are as follows:

• Delhi Dada Dadi Help Foundation helpline: +(91)-9212717171 | 9212050505 | 26260777

• Madhya Pradesh Dada Dadi helpline: 99778 85999

• Hyderabad Senior Citizen Helpline 0901 047 0724 Prasanthi Karunamaya-Organisation

• Telangana government helpline for senior citizens 14567

Note that 14567 is registered as a nationwide helpline for senior citizens. It is worth trying it from any city even if not in Telangana, to see if it is functional.

7.5 List of helplines for essential goods delivery during the Covid pandemic

A list of helplines for senior citizens for getting essential deliveries of food during the Covid pandemic lockdown is given here:

https://www.thebetterindia.com/221785/coronavirus-india-covid19-senior-citizen-helpline-number-delivery-food-medicine-emergency-tan42/

NGOs working with Senior citizens

In this chapter, we discuss a few of the main NGOs that are working to help senior citizens in India. Many of these NGOs run their own helplines for senior citizens in different cities. A senior citizen can either call them, email them or walk into their offices and chat to the counsellors about their problems including abuse. They provide a sympathetic and patient hearing to the problems of senior citizens specifically, and so fulfil a vital social function.

Give the variety of problems faced by senior citizens, the NGOs can be a very valuable source of support. The helplines run by the NGOs complement the police run helplines. The NGOs typically provide support and counselling for all aspects of the senior citizens' lives, not just in cases of abuse. Their support extends to the mental and physical health issues, financial issues, legal issues, destitution, homelessness, property disputes and so on.

8.1 HelpAge India

HelpAge India is one of the largest NGOs working for the welfare of senior citizens. They were established in 1978, run a variety of programs for senior citizens. Their programs include cancer care, cataract surgeries, supporting destitute elders, running senior citizen helplines etc. They have contacts among police and lawyers who can assist the senior citizens in legal cases. They have run numerous surveys and compiled reports of the extent of the problem of senior citizen abuse in India.

They have branches in different cities of India, with the main branch in New Delhi. They have collaborations with other international organizations working to help the elderly. They have won numerous awards for their activities, including Bharat Nirman Award, 2020 UN Population Award and Times Social Impact Award.

Head Office address: Address: 17, Tara Crescent Road, Qutab Institutional Area, New Delhi, 110016, Delhi, India Phone: +91 11 4168 8955

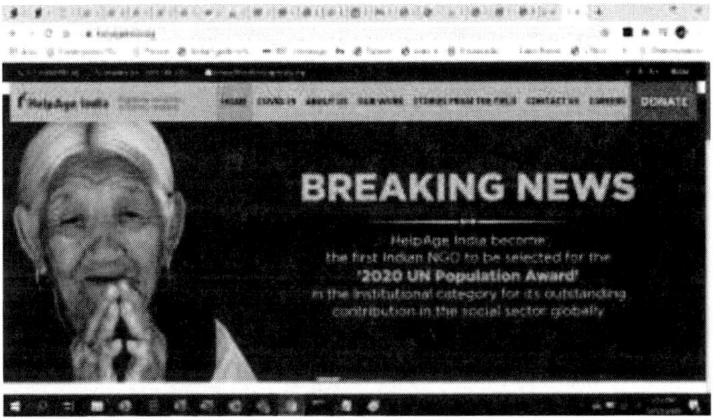

Figure 10: Homepage of the HelpAge India website

Links to websites for more information

- https://www.helpageindia.org/
- https://en.wikipedia.org/wiki/HelpAge_India

8.2 Dignity Foundation

Dignity foundation was established in 1995 in Mumbai, originally starting as a magazine called Dignity Dialogue. and now have branches in many cities. They also run city specific helplines for senior citizens in six cities. They run a wide variety of programs benefitting senior citizens.

Head office address: Dignity Foundation, B-206, 2nd Floor, Byculla Service Industries Premises Sussex Road, Byculla (E) Mumbai - 400 027

Telephone : 6138 1100

Email : responsedignity@dignityfoundation.com

Websites : www.dignityfoundation.com / www.dignitylifestyle.org

8.3 Agewell Foundation

Agewell Foundation has association NGO status with UN DPI. It was set up in 1999. They run various activities like healthcare campaigns and training programs. They conduct research into the problems faced by senior citizens, as well as advocate for welfare measures for senior citizens. They interact with over 25000 senior citizens on a daily basis.

Office address: M-8A, Lajpat Nagar-II, New Delhi-110024, India

Phone : +91-29836486, +91-29840484, +91-29830005

Fax : 011-29840484

E-mail : agewellfoundation@gmail.com

Website : www.agewellfoundation.org

8.4 Dada Dadi

Dada Dadi is an organization for senior citizens that is based in Chandigarh. It runs various helplines and advocacy on behalf of senior citizens. It has a very comprehensive website with a good listing of rights and support services available for senior citizens in India.

Website: https://www.dadadadi.org/

8.5 Harmony

This organization was initially launched in 2004 as a magazine called Harmony magazine, which is still running. It is based in Mumbai.

Website: https://www.harmonyindia.org/

8.6 List of other organizations

A list of a few other NGOs is as below. However there are many other NGOs too for senior citizens, as well as many NGO who might not be specifically for senior citizens, also work for their welfare.

• Devamitra foundation https://www.devamitra.org/old-age-ngo-india/

• Sneh foundation https://www.facebook.com/Sneh-Foundation-136083433482227/

Problems in Accessing Help and Strategies to Overcome the Problems

In this chapter, we discuss a few problems and obstacles that senior citizens commonly face when they try to report abuse to the authorities. We also cover a few legal strategies that senior citizens can use to protect themselves and overcome the problems.

9.1 Problems with police

Many times, the police are reluctant to file FIRs or act on the abuse complaints, even when abuse is reported by senior citizens.

This may be due to several reasons such as the following:

- Corruption by the police
- Police wanting to avoid extra work
- Abuser being an influential person
- Police wanting to take bribes from the abused senior citizen before filing any case
- Police having taken bribes from the abusers

• Reported crime details from the senior citizens being vague

• Police believing it is difficult to collect evidence for the alleged crimes by the senior citizens

• Alleged crime not being in the police station jurisdiction

• Police not sensitized to take senior citizens seriously

• Police concluding non cognizable offence without a proper investigation

For example, in case of abuse of senior citizens related to ongoing property disputes, the police may close the case and not act citing that property disputes are beyond their jurisdiction.

Given that senior citizens are often reluctant to approach the police for several reasons, this perceived or real inaction by the police can have a doubly adverse effect on the reporting and prevention of senior citizen abuse. Hence, it should be combated.

9.1.1 Example where police did not take senior citizen abuse complaints seriously

The following extract from a newspaper shows how police inaction may work in case of senior citizen abuse, and a possible remedy to approach the courts to force the police to act.

The Hindu, Dec 21, 2020: Delhi HC orders police protection for senior citizen couple. Duo claims assault by daughter, her husband

The Delhi High Court has ordered the city police to ensure sufficient protection for a senior citizen couple who claimed that they were being "tormented and physically beaten" by their daughter and son-in-law living with them.

Justice Vibhu Bakhru said the couple can also approach their area District Magistrate under Rule 22 of Delhi Maintenance and Welfare of Parents and Senior Citizens Rules (DMWPSCR) for their protection. Rule 22 of DMWPSCR lays down guidelines for protection of life and property of senior citizens. It says that complaints of senior citizens shall be promptly attended to by the local police.

'Police inaction': The High Court's order came while hearing the plea of a 67-year-old man and his wife who said the police have not taken any effective steps to protect them despite several complaints. The man, who claimed to be suffering from paralysis and old-age ailments, said that on October 12 he was beaten up by his daughter. He had called the police and some officers had visited the premises. However, they did not take any action and asked the couple to submit a written complaint. He alleged that their statements were also not recorded. Thereafter, on December 13, his daughter and son-in-law once again assaulted them, claimed the complainant. The Delhi government's Additional Standing Counsel submitted that the complaints received from the old couple do not reflect any cognisable offence and are largely regarding unpleasantness and petty squabbles between the family members. The counsel, however, assured the court that the concerned beat staff will visit the complainants' residence on a daily basis and ensure that they are not brought to any harm.

9.1.2 Strategies with the police

In case the police do not register complaints properly without investigation or else close the complaints too soon, the following strategies can be used by senior citizens and their well-wishers:

- Approach senior citizen cells, if available in their city

- File Right to Information Requests (RTIs) to the inspectors or higher up police officers, to get the police to act on their specific complaints of abuse

- Always file written complaints to the police rather than verbal

- If possible, collect evidence of abuse, such as video or audio clips, hospital reports of injuries from a government hospital

- Send the complaints to the police and other agencies by registered post or speed post, keeping a record of their sending

- Approach the courts to force the police to register FIRs

- Approach the senior citizens NGOs, such as HelpAge India or Dignity Foundation, for help

- Approach the National Commission for Women (NCW) in case of non-action by the police and if the abused is a woman

• Approach the National Human Rights Commission India (NHRC) with evidence of past correspondence and non-action by the police

9.2 Problems with helplines

Although it is good that helplines are available for abused senior citizens in different cities of India, however they suffer from some practical problems. Some of the problems are as follows:

• Often, the senior citizens might not be able to articulate the problem of abuse accurately.

• Senior citizens may suffer from memory loss and not be able to recount events of abuse accurately.

• Senior citizens may not be able to collect evidence about the abuse, given their lack of familiarity with technology.

• Since the senior citizens are often living with and dependent on the abuser, they may not tell the full story for fear of the abuse becoming worse.

• Senior citizens may be currently scared of threats made by the abusers, who may be their family members, even if they are not living with them.

• Sometimes the police might be reluctant to lodge FIRs or take action, even after the abuse is reported.

• In some cities, especially the smaller cities, the police might be corrupt and take bribes from the abusers and suppress the investigation.

• In some cases, the abusers may be influential people who may be able to put pressure on the police.

• Helplines run by the NGOs, since they do not have official powers and are not directly linked to the police, might not be able to do much in case of abuses or threats, other than reporting the abuse to the local police.

Given all the above issues, it is important for the persons running the helplines to be extra sensitive to the senior citizens issues, give them a patient hearing and the best advice to move forward to prevent the abuse.

9.2.1 Strategies with the helplines

The following can be some strategies to follow if a call to the helpline number, especially if the helpline is run by the police, is not useful:

• Follow up the helpline call with a written complaint

• Send the written complaint by registered post/ speed post and email.

• Contact the police senior citizen cell, if it exists

• Follow the other strategies as mentioned in the previous section in case of problems with the police

9.3 Problems with lawyers and judiciary

Sometimes the abused senior citizen may have no option but to take the help of the judiciary to enforce their rights and prevent abuse. This can be necessary in case of property disputes, such as when a son or neighbor is trying to take hold of the property by force, or in case of wills. This can also be needed when the police do not act on a written complaint by the senior citizen. In such cases, the senior citizen may have to hire a lawyer to send a legal notice or file a case on the abuser.

However, hiring a lawyer or filing a case may lead to several problems of its own, including the following:

- Senior citizen may not know the legal process and depend completely on the lawyer

- Lawyer may overcharge the senior citizen

- The lawyer may accept bribes from the abusive party and misrepresent the case

- Lawyer may be incompetent or inexperienced

- Lawyer may treat the senior citizen as an easy income source and not take the case seriously

- Lawyer may advise the senior citizen to file multiple unnecessary cases, just because they get extra money per filing

- The property dispute cases may continue for months or years

• While the case is going on in the courts, there is no respite for the senior citizen and the abuses may continue

9.3.1 Strategies with the lawyers

Some of the strategies for senior citizens to prevent the problems with the lawyers are as follows:

• Consult several lawyers before deciding to hire one

• Put the case or abuse details on an online site like lawrato.com to get the opinions of various lawyers

• Hire a lawyer who has some experience, if possible check their credentials or qualifications online

• Hire lawyers who are familiar with technology and keeps themselves abreast of the latest developments, ideally they should not be too old

• Hire lawyers who do the case work themselves rather than relying on too many assistants

• Negotiate the rate with the lawyer in advance and insist on paying in installments, dependent on the progression of the case

• In case the lawyer pressurizes the senior citizens to settle or to file extra cases, the senior citizens should do their own research before deciding, by consulting multiple people

• Make yourself familiar with the court process by visiting courts, talking to people, reading past judgments and so on.

9.4. Use of RTI Act

The Right to Information Act (RTI), 2015 is an Act of the Parliament of India "to provide for setting out the practical regime of right to information for citizens." The RTI Act allows citizens of India, including senior citizens, to request information from any public authority about its work and actions. This act is a very useful tool that can be used by senior citizens in case of inaction by police or other institutions in response to reports of abuse or other problems. It must be noted that the RTI act is mainly applicable for public data, such as data in the public domain or data related to actions by government officials or police. It cannot be used generally for data related to private companies

The act comprises filing an RTI application (online or on paper) with the correct authority (state or central government) on whom the information request is to be made. There is a time limit within which the authority has to respond to the information request under RTI, and the person can file an appeal if they are not satisfied with the response.

For example, in case of inaction by the police to a written complaint of abuse, a senior citizen can file an RTI to the inspector or concerned police official, or their seniors, asking what action has been taken to their specific complaints. This puts pressure on the police or other authorities to act.

Some links to get more information on RTI and the process, are as follows:

- Wikipedia. Right to Information Act 2005 https://en.wikipedia.org/wiki/Right_to_Information_Act,_2005

- Information about RTI from experts https://onlinerti.com/about-rti

- Online RTI website https://www.rtionline.gov.in/

Some practical tips

In this chapter, we discuss a few general tips on how to help or enable senior citizens to report abuse and protect themselves from abuse.

10.1 Awareness of rights of senior citizens

One of the things people can do to help their senior citizen relatives from threats and abuses is to make them aware of their rights and options for help, including police helpline numbers in various cities such as 1090. Same goes for awareness of the laws that protect them, such as the senior citizens protection act.

10.2 Training to use technology

Another way to help the senior citizens is to make them familiar with technology. This can include the following:

• Teaching them how to access the internet

• Teaching them to browse basic websites to find information

• Making sure they have internet on their smartphones and know how to use it etc.

10.3 Making senior citizens aware of helplines and other support

Another way to help senior citizens is to make them aware of the helplines, as well as give them a list of helpline numbers to call, such as numbers of NGOs, whenever an issue such as abuse occurs.

10.4 Changing ingrained mindsets among senior citizens

Changing ingrained mindsets of senior citizens, such as decreasing their ingrained fear of police and courts by gently explaining the procedures to approach them, can also go a long way for them to asset their rights and curb abuse by others. Same goes for awareness of things such as writing and registering a will for their property.

10.5 Avoiding domestic abuse

For married children of senior citizens, one of the ways of protecting their parents from abuse by their wives or other relatives can be simply to move out to a different house close by, yet ensuring that their parents have enough support when it comes to basic needs such as medical and psychological needs.

10.6 Education to change mindsets of young people

Young people can also be educated about the problems faced by older people. Such education can go a long way in solving inter generation conflicts and reducing the possibility of abuse of senior citizens.

Conclusion

In this book, we have looked at a few problems facing senior citizens in India, especially that of abuse and ill treatment by family members.

Reporting and combating abuse of senior citizens wherever we see it is only the first step.

11.1 Longer term solutions

The longer term solution for the problem of elder abuse is to raise awareness in society, show senior citizens in a positive light and highlight their problems, so that such incidents are prevented. This goes hand in hand with a better equipped health system to take care of the medical needs of senior citizens. Legal institutions have to be strengthened, along with simplified special court procedures, to make sure senior citizens face no difficulty in accessing legal help whenever they need it.

11.2 What the government can do

The government can play its role by increased support to senior citizens and sensitization of government employees, especially those who atre serivice providers, to the problems faced by senior citizens. They should ensure the helplines are available in all cities big or small. There should be monitoring of the efficiency of the helplines to make sure they are effective in preventing abuse of different kinds. There should be increased government funding to senior citizens organizations, old age homes and NGOs, aswell as in areas like healthcare and a comprehensive medical insurance for senior citizens. Schemes for digitalization should keep in mind their potential impact on senior citizens who may not know technology.

11.3 Change in social attitudes

Many of the problems of elder abuse have its roots in other social problems, such as poverty, unemployment, lack of living spaces, inter generational gaps. To combat them we have to take responsibility as a society. The media, film industry, arts, and other industries have to play their part in highlighting the problems of modern lifestyles in which senior citizens often get caught up.

Abuse of senior citizens is a problem for all of us, and so we have to try and combat it together. Only by getting together and fighting the senior citizens abuse and taking steps to protect our senior citizens, can we make a better society in India.